MW01177811

Ocean Diving

Traveling Through Inner Space

by W. Wright Robinson

Perfection Learning® CA

I would like to dedicate this book to the incredible "Crew" whose wit has helped keep me going. Thank you!

Designer: Jan M. Michalson
Inside Illustration: Dea Marks
Photographs courtesy of Corbis: pp 37, 38, 49, 52

About the Author

W. Wright Robinson holds a master's degree in biology. He is a former instructor of biological oceanography as well as a biological researcher. He has a keen interest in oceanography and places a high value on communicating his love and knowledge of the ocean to children. Mr. Robinson is also the author of *Incredible Facts About the Ocean, Volumes I, II, and III*, published by Dillon Press.

Explaining his approach, the author states, "By using a question-and-answer format, each topic is explained in a way that allows the information to build gradually through a logical progression of questions. In this way, the student is guided through complex principles, learning not only the answers to questions, but also what questions to ask."

Mr. Robinson currently teaches biology, field ecology, and advanced-placement environmental science at Charlotte Country Day School in Charlotte, North Carolina.

Printed in the United States of America. For information, contact Perfection Learning® Corporation, 1000 North Second Avenue, P.O. Box 500, Logan, Iowa 51546-1099.
PB ISBN-13: 978-0-7891-1956-8 ISBN-10: 0-7891-1956-0
RLB ISBN-13: 978-0-7807-6141-4 ISBN-10: 0-7807-6141-3
10 11 12 13 14 15 PP 12 11 10 09 08 07

Table of Contents

Skin Diving/ Scuba Diving

What is skin diving?

A skin diver is a swimmer wearing a mask, swim fins, and a snorkel. The mask keeps water out of the diver's eyes. That way he can see better underwater.

The fins give the diver webbed feet, like a frog. Fins help him move faster and with more control.

The snorkel is a hollow, J-shaped tube. It is 12 to 14 inches long. The short curved end goes into the mouth. The straight section sticks out above the water. Air passes through the snorkel. Then the swimmer can breathe underwater.

A skin diver can dive deep under the water, holding his breath. But he can only stay down until he has to take another breath.

A diver with a mask and snorkel stays on the surface. He can have his face in the water as long as he wants.

What is scuba diving?

A **scuba** (SKOO-bah) diver wears a mask, swim fins, and a snorkel, just like a skin diver. The scuba diver also carries a tank of air on her back. This air lets the diver breathe underwater.

Most scuba divers breathe the same air we breathe. The air is forced into the scuba tank under great pressure. The air is squeezed, or **compressed,** into the tank. It is called compressed air.

Most scuba divers use a **weight belt**. This is needed because most people float in water. The weights on the belt keep the diver underwater.

It is important that the scuba diver not wear too many weights. It would be too hard to swim back to the surface.

Another piece of scuba diving gear is the **buoyancy compensator** (**BC**). The BC attaches to the tank. It fastens with straps around the diver's chest and stomach.

The BC can be filled with air from the tank. This makes it easy for the diver to float. But the BC does even more. Divers can control the amount of air in the BC. This helps them return slowly to the surface.

The BC can also keep a diver at one depth beneath the waves. With the right amount of air in the BC, a diver can hang in mid-water. The diver won't float up or sink deeper.

What does *scuba* mean?

The word *scuba* stands for *S*elf-*C*ontained *U*nderwater *B*reathing *A*pparatus. These words tell us that scuba is a device, or **apparatus.** It allows us to breathe underwater.

Scuba divers can breathe underwater. They can swim freely below the waves. They can go wherever they choose.

You can become a scuba diver by taking classes from an instructor. You will learn some things in a classroom. And you will learn some things in a swimming pool.

As you will see from reading this book, there is much to learn about scuba diving.

How does the air get out of a scuba tank?

A **regulator** is at the top of a scuba tank. It controls or *regulates* the flow of air from the tank.

A hose connects the regulator to the diver's mouth. By sucking on a **mouthpiece** at the end of the hose, the diver gets air from the tank. The air travels through the hose and into the mouth as it is needed.

Then when divers breathe out, or exhale, their air forms bubbles. The air bubbles rise to the surface.

How long can a scuba diver stay underwater?

This answer depends on many things. For one, divers breathe faster when they are excited, cold, or working hard. So they use their air more quickly than when they are warm and relaxed.

It also depends on the kind of scuba tank used. Not all tanks are the same size. Sometimes divers wear twins, or two tanks.

Usually, a scuba diver can stay at a depth of 30 feet for about one hour. This is on a single, standard tank of air and good conditions.

Divers wear special watches. The watches let them know how long they have been down.

They must also know how much longer they can stay down. For this, a pressure **gauge** is attached to the scuba tank. As the air in the tank is used for breathing, the pressure goes down. The pressure gauge shows how much air is left in the tank.

How deep can skin divers and scuba divers go?

Well-trained skin divers can hold their breath a long time. They can dive down 80 to 100 feet. This distance equals 25 to 35 yards on a football field.

A scuba diver (breathing ordinary compressed air) should not go down more than 130 feet. This distance, almost 45 yards, doesn't seem like much at a football game. But when you are underwater, it's a long way down.

Any diver going this deep must be well trained. The diver must be experienced with deep-water diving. And she must be in very good physical condition.

It is important for a diver to know how far down she has gone. A depth gauge will tell her. This gauge is often worn on the diver's wrist, like a watch.

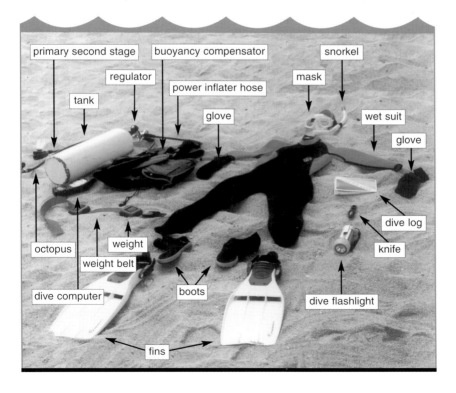

Why is there so much pressure underwater?

To answer this question, we need to begin at the surface of the ocean. The air around us forms the **atmosphere** in which we live. This atmosphere of gases is over 100 miles thick.

The force of gravity holds you on the ground. Gravity also pulls on the air. Gravity gives both you and the air weight.

The weight of all this air presses on you. It presses on every square inch of your body. (A square inch is a square that is one inch on each side.)

15 pounds

Pressure at sea level

At the surface of the ocean, the pressure of the air is almost 15 pounds. That's 15 pounds on every square inch of your body. This is called one atmosphere of pressure. You don't feel this pressure because you are used to it.

Below the ocean surface, gravity pulls on the water too. For every 33 feet you dive down, another atmosphere of pressure, or 15 pounds of pressure, is added. So at 66 feet, there are three atmospheres of pressure. There's the one at the surface, the one at 33 feet, and the one at 66 feet. So at 99 feet there are four atmospheres.

60 pounds

Pressure at 99 feet below sea level
(4 x 15 = 60)

Why do your ears feel stuffy or stopped up when you go underwater?

Do your ears ever feel funny when you dive to the bottom of a swimming pool? Do they feel strange when you go up in an elevator or airplane?

The part of the ear we see is called the external ear. It directs sound waves into the tube that leads inside your head. This tube is called the auditory canal.

The eardrum is at the end of this canal. The eardrum is a thin sheet of tissue. It is tightly stretched. This makes it vibrate when sound hits it.

But the eardrum does something else. It forms a thin wall between the atmosphere outside your head and the air space inside your ear.

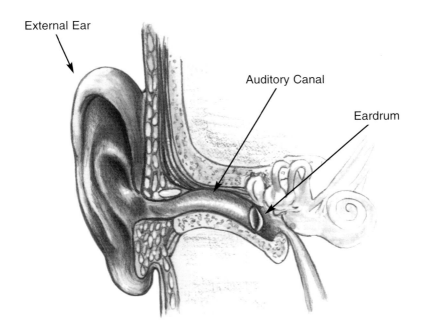

External Ear

Auditory Canal

Eardrum

As you swim down, the pressure increases outside your body. But the pressure in the space behind your eardrum stays the same.

The greater, outside pressure pushes in on the eardrum. It tries to get behind it. This makes your ears feel stuffy. The stuffy feeling will stay until you can get the pressure equal on both sides of your eardrum.

You may wonder what will happen if you try to go deeper. Your eardrum will begin to hurt. If you ignore the pain and continue down, your eardrum could tear.

When your eardrum tears, you lose your hearing. Blood from the torn drum will trickle out of the auditory canal. Your ear bleeds!

Caution: *Never wear earplugs when scuba diving. The pressure underwater could push the earplug through your eardrum.*

How can you protect your ears from damage underwater?

It is easy to protect your ears from damage underwater. A tube connects the space behind the eardrum to your throat. This is called the **auditory tube**.

You can pass air from your throat through this tube and into the air space behind the drum. This will make the pressure equal on both sides of the eardrum.

Just swallow or move your jaw around to make the pressure equal. If this doesn't work, an instructor can show you other ways to equalize the pressure.

What happens if you dive too deep?

The air you breathe becomes harmful as you travel down farther and farther beneath the waves. Under pressure, **nitrogen**

in the air begins to affect you like a drug.

You begin to feel that everything is great. Even when it is not. Your fears are forgotten. You get a relaxed feeling. It is like breathing nitrous oxide, or laughing gas, at a dentist's office.

The maximum safe scuba diving depth is 130 feet. But nitrogen can cause trouble way before 130 feet deep. Experienced divers say that at just 100 feet they cannot always trust themselves.

Oxygen can also be a problem for deep-water divers. This life-giving gas becomes toxic, or poisonous, under high pressure. Oxygen poisoning affects the brain. It can cause **convulsions**. The oxygen in the air we breathe can even kill at greater depths.

To be safe, divers breathe special gas mixtures when they go deep underwater. They also need the special mixture when they must stay under for a long time.

What is a "special gas" mixture?

You will remember that breathing too much oxygen or nitrogen in deep water can cause big problems for a diver. But there's a way to prevent these problems.

Special gas mixtures are made. They change the amount of oxygen or nitrogen being breathed. Different depths require different mixtures. The way the gases are mixed depends upon how deep the diver needs to go.

Some of the commonly used special gas mixtures include
 • trimix—a special mix of oxygen, helium, and nitrogen.
 • nitrox—oxygen and nitrogen mixed in amounts not found in normal air.
 • heliox—a mixture in which a small amount of oxygen is added to helium. Helium does not cause the problems that nitrogen can.

What will happen if you come up too fast?

Let's use an example to answer this question. When you open a can or bottle of soda pop, it fizzes. Bubbles rise out of the liquid. This is because the carbonation (a gas) was added to the liquid under pressure.

As long as the top stays on the can or bottle, the pressure inside remains high. This pressure holds the gas in the liquid. But as soon as the top comes off, the pressure is released. The gas rushes out. This causes the familiar "pssssst" we hear when we open a can of soda.

When you are scuba diving, the story is the same. Your blood is like the soda pop. It can hold more air (gas) under pressure than it can at the surface.

When you breathe air underwater, the pressure pushes more gas into your blood than it does at the surface. If you rise from the bottom too fast, the gas in your blood bubbles out.

With less pressure, the blood cannot hold as much gas. The gas must come out.

The result of having gas bubbles in your blood can vary. It may only be a mild pain. Or the problems can be much worse. In some cases, the bubbles cause extreme pain or even death. This is called decompression sickness. It's more commonly known as *the bends*.

How can you protect yourself from the bends?

It is easy to protect yourself from the bends. The easiest way is to come back up to the surface slowly.

Remember, there is more air (gas) in your blood. So it will take longer to come out. If you come to the surface slowly, your lungs have time to remove the extra gas. When you breathe out, this gas passes from your body safely. Bubbles do not form in your blood.

Sport divers don't dive below 130 feet. They can't stay very long at this depth. The deeper a diver goes, the shorter the time he can stay down.

Divers use computers or special dive tables to tell them how long they can stay down at different depths. It is important for a diver not to exceed the time or depth on the computer or table. If that happens, decompression stops will be needed. Diving longer or deeper than the table says is very dangerous.

The following table shows the maximum time a diver can stay down at different depths. This information is from the YMCA dive table for sport divers.

Depth		Total Bottom Time/minutes
meters	feet	
4.5	15	350
6	20	325
7.5	25	315
9	30	250
10.5	35	220
12	40	150
15	50	80
18	60	50
21	70	40
24	80	30
27	90	25
30	100	20
33	110	13
36	120	10
39	130	5

Notice that there is a break between 100 feet and 110 feet. Most sport divers never dive deeper than 100 feet. Also notice that the time says total bottom time. This time is for the first dive of the day.

For example, if a diver goes 60 feet deep for 50 minutes, he can't dive again that day. But if he goes to 60 feet for 20 minutes and rests for a while, he can do another shorter or shallower dive. The complete dive table tells him how long he must rest and how long he can stay down next time.

What is meant by *decompression?*

In the section "What is scuba diving?" we learned about compressed air. It is normal air that has been squeezed into a scuba tank. Pressure was used to compress the air in the tank. When we *de*compress the air, we remove or let off the pressure.

Sometimes divers must go deep or stay down for a long time. If so, they can't just rise slowly to the surface. There is too much gas in their blood.

These divers must stop for several minutes at certain depths. They are called decompression stops. These stops give the blood enough time to carry the extra gas to the lungs. There it is released.

What happens if the air runs out when you are 100 feet underwater?

You shouldn't scuba dive alone. Dive with a **buddy,** if possible. Then if you run out of air, you can share the air in your buddy's tank. Just take turns breathing from the same tank as you rise slowly to the surface.

In an emergency, a trained scuba diver can return to the

surface without an air tank. Imagine a diver 66 feet below the surface. Remember, this person is exposed to three atmospheres of pressure.

The first atmosphere of pressure comes from the air above the ocean. A second atmosphere of pressure is added by the first 33 feet of water. And the third atmosphere is added by the second 33 feet of water. So three atmospheres of pressure are felt 66 feet below the waves.

The extra pressure at 66 feet pushes the tiny particles of air close together inside your lungs. They are closer than they would be at the surface. So if you take a deep breath 66 feet underwater, more air particles go into your lungs than if you were on the surface.

As you begin to rise toward the surface, there is less water overhead. Less water means less pressure. With less pressure, the air in your lungs expands.

When this happens, you don't need to breathe in (inhale). Your lungs are already full of air. You *must*, however, remember to breathe out (exhale) all the way to the surface. Otherwise your lungs could swell and explode like a balloon.

Caution: *When scuba diving, never hold your breath when returning to the surface.*

What can you do if your mask comes off underwater?

If your mask gets knocked off underwater, remain calm. Put the mask back on.

Turn so that you are upright in the water. Your head will be toward the surface. Your feet will be toward the bottom.

In this position, press on the top of the mask and blow through your nose. The air leaving your nose will fill the mask. It pushes the water out the bottom of the mask.

It is not unusual for water to flood the mask. Sometimes a diver lets water inside on purpose. The water washes away fog that can build up on the face plate.

What is a diving flag used for?

A red flag with a white diagonal stripe is called a Diver Down flag. This flag is attached to a float on the surface. It tells people driving boats that divers are under the water. When boaters see this flag, they should stay away.

What is a wet suit?

A wet suit allows water to pass through it. This tight-fitting rubber or **neoprene** suit traps a thin layer of water against the skin. Here your body heat quickly warms the water. This warm water helps keep you warm.

What is a dry suit?

A dry suit, as the name tells us, keeps the diver dry underwater. This leakproof rubber suit is used in places like the North and South Poles. There the water is extremely cold.

A dry suit is also worn by a sport diver when the water temperature is below 60°F. To stay warm, you must wear a dry suit over wool or thermal underwear.

Is diving dangerous?

Diving *can* be dangerous. But it does not have to be. To be a diver, you must take classes from an instructor. You must pass tests. These tests show that you know how to avoid dangers.

In this chapter, we learned that breathing the wrong gas mixture can be harmful. Rising too fast from the bottom also can be harmful.

Now we will move on to chapter 2. There we'll discover some of the dangerous animals that you could face as a diver. The end of chapter 2 explains dangers that most people never think about. This knowledge could help prevent unnecessary suffering. Or it could even save your life one day.

Danger Beneath the Waves

What living dangers do you face in the water?

Danger comes in many forms, living and nonliving. It often comes quickly and without warning. Being aware can prepare you for trouble. It could save your life.

We will first learn how a diver's life is threatened by animals that can bite, sting, or shock a person to death. A **shark** is one example. This is a *living* danger.

Let's begin with the much-feared SHARK.

How dangerous is a shark?

The answer to this question depends upon the shark. These fish are not all the same. Over 250 kinds of sharks live in the ocean. Fewer than 20 of these are known to attack humans.

The kinds of sharks that threaten divers are large and strong. They are very good swimmers. They are at home in the water, and people aren't. Also, sharks are amazing hunters. Now you have the setting for a possible threat.

Sharks can be dangerous. They have large mouths, strong jaws, and sharp teeth. Bites from these fish are severe.

Sharks are meat-eaters. And people are meat. So sharks should always be treated with respect.

It is hard to know just how dangerous sharks are to divers. Many thousands of people dive each year. Of these divers, very few have been attacked by sharks.

Most shark attacks involve surface swimmers, not scuba divers. Also, sharks do not kill all the people they attack. Many shark-attack victims live.

In spite of movies and stories, sharks are not our most common enemy in the ocean. There are other more dangerous animals. They injure far more people than do sharks.

What are some other dangerous animals in the water?

There are many different animals in the water that can injure or kill humans. The shark may be the most feared fish in the sea. But the barracuda is easily in second place.

Some of the other animals to keep an eye out for are **stingrays**, some **jellyfish**, and **moray eels**. They are not as feared as sharks and barracuda. But these sea creatures can be dangerous.

Far more people have painful encounters with stingrays, jellyfish, and morays than with sharks and barracuda combined.

What is a barracuda?

A barracuda is a fish. There are over 20 kinds of barracuda. Only one of these is dangerous to divers. It is the **great barracuda**.

This long, slender fish may grow 8 to 10 feet long. It is usually dark green or blue on top. It has silver or yellow sides and a white belly. Dark bars mark the back and sides. Its mouth is large and filled with long, knife-like teeth.

The great barracuda is built for speed. So this fish can attack quickly and fiercely.

Like sharks, great barracuda rarely attack underwater swimmers.

How can you protect yourself from sharks and barracuda?

There are no rules that will protect you from an attack by sharks or the great barracuda. These fish are hard to predict. You can never be sure what they are going to do.

There are, however, some things that should NOT be done. Divers should not wear shiny equipment or jewelry. It will attract these fish.

If blood is in the water, leave the area. Both sharks and barracuda are attracted by blood from fish or divers.

It is also dangerous to dive in muddy water. In clear water, a diver has a better chance. He can see well, so he can avoid an accidental bite.

If you meet a shark or barracuda, you should slowly swim away. Swim backward. Keep facing the threatening fish. Stay underwater. Do not swim on the surface.

Remember, most attacks involve surface swimmers, not scuba divers. Once you reach the shore or your boat, get out of the water. Do this as quickly as possible.

Do stingrays really sting?

Yes, they do really sting. Stingrays are round or kite-shaped, flat-bodied fish. They can cause very painful injuries to divers and swimmers. But it is not a stingray's mouth that can hurt you.

A stingray has a long, thin, whip-like tail. It uses its tail to defend itself. This tail has a sharp, pointed spine. The spine can easily cut through a person's skin. Poison covers the spine. It enters the wound and causes a stinging pain.

Stingrays do not attack divers. These fish sometimes lie on the bottom in shallow water. Most people are hurt when they wade into the water. By mistake, they step on the hard, poisonous spine.

Other people are hurt by stingrays when they step on the fish itself. The ray whips its tail around. It drives the sharp spine into the victim's ankle or the top of the foot.

Stingray wounds often get infected. They should always be treated by a doctor.

How can jellyfish hurt a diver?

There are over 200 kinds of jellyfish. Most of them have a very weak sting. It is so weak that people never feel it. But some jellyfish can give very painful stings.

The box jellyfish (also called the sea wasp) lives near Australia. It can kill a person within four minutes. The pain is said to be unbearable.

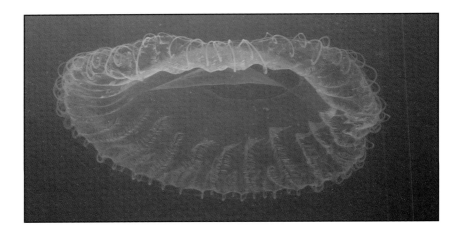

When you see jellyfish in the water, be careful. Wear protective clothing. This can be a wet suit or dry suit. You can even wear long underwear. Also wear socks and gloves. Just be sure to cover yourself.

It is best to stay out of the water when you see jellyfish. It's hard to believe that jellyfish can cause so much pain. They look fragile and helpless. But watch out. They can hurt!

Most jellyfish have glassy-looking, umbrella-shaped bodies. Below their bodies hang **tentacles**. The tentacles are like threads. The tentacles give the sting.

Most people who brush against a jellyfish feel a mild sting. Their skin might feel prickly. This happens where the tentacles touch them. Worse stings cause a burning, throbbing pain. Serious stings can leave the victim unconscious.

In severe cases, the victim may have muscle cramps. He may begin vomiting. And he may have a loss of speech. In some cases, the victim can have problems breathing. He may go into convulsions. He can even die.

Just how serious a jellyfish sting is depends on three things:
(1) the kind of jellyfish,
(2) how large an area of skin it has stung,
(3) and whether the person is allergic to the sting.

How do jellyfish sting someone?

Jellyfish have special *stinging cells* that do the job. Millions of these tiny cells are lined up, side by side. They run down the tentacles that hang from the animal's body.

Each stinging cell has a pointed, hollow tube. The tube is coiled inside the cell. Liquid fills the space around the tube. A small, hair-like trigger is outside each stinging cell. When something touches this trigger, the top of the cell pops open.

The hollow tube fires out. Its sharp, pointed tip sticks the target. The liquid inside the stinging cell moves through the tube. It enters the poor victim. It is this liquid that causes the stinging pain.

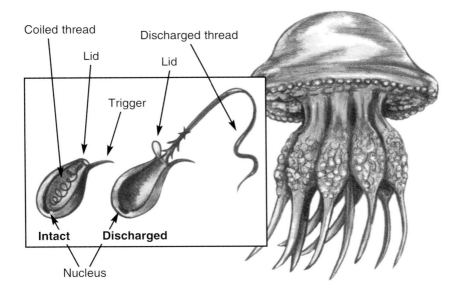

Coiled thread
Discharged thread
Lid
Lid
Trigger
Intact
Discharged
Nucleus

This is what happens when someone swims into the tentacles of a jellyfish. Imagine thousands—or maybe even hundreds of thousands—of stinging cells firing. All the cells send their poison into the victim. The result can be very, very painful.

Are there any snakes living in the ocean?

Yes, there are about 50 kinds of sea snakes. They live in warm, tropical waters. They live in the Indian and Pacific oceans.

These snakes are not the same shape as snakes on land. Most land snakes are long and narrow. They have pointed tails.

A sea snake is also long and narrow. But its tail is flat, like the tail of a fish. By moving its flat tail from side to side, a sea snake can move. It can easily move forward in water. It can even move backward through the water.

Whether they live on land or in the ocean, all snakes breathe air. All snakes have lungs. Sea snakes must hold their breath when they swim underwater. This is not a problem. Sea snakes can stay underwater for several hours at a time.

When hungry, some sea snakes move along the bottom. They search for small fish to eat. Other sea snakes do something else. They lie still on top of the water. They look like sticks floating on the surface. Small fish come to rest in the shade below these "sticks." They are quickly caught. They are usually eaten head first.

Are sea snakes poisonous?

Some sea snakes have **venom**. This venom is poisonous. It is 50 times worse than the venom of a deadly king cobra. This makes sea snakes some of the most poisonous snakes in the world. Divers should avoid them.

If a diver is bitten by a sea snake, she should lie still. She should be taken to a doctor immediately.

If possible, the snake should be caught. It should also go to the doctor. It needs to be identified so the victim can get proper treatment.

Is an eel some kind of sea snake?

No. Eels may look like snakes. But eels are actually long, slender fish. If you look closely at an eel, you will see that it has fins and gills. Sea snakes have neither.

Ocean divers must keep an eye out for moray eels. And divers need to watch for electric eels in some rivers.

How dangerous are moray eels?

If left alone, moray eels probably won't attack a diver. Most injuries occur when divers bother eels. They reach into holes or

under rocks and coral. This is where these eels hide.

Eels don't see well. When a hand enters its hiding place, the eel may think it is a small fish. Or the eel may think it is an attacker. Either way, the result is often the same. The eel strikes. Its powerful jaws have strong, knife-like teeth. They can cause serious damage to an arm or hand.

Are electric eels really "electric"?

Yes. Electric eels can produce a powerful electric shock. This shock can kill some animals. It can stun a full-grown man. It can even stun a horse.

Eels have special electric organs in their bodies. There are chemicals within the cells and tissues of these organs. These chemicals produce the electricity. The animal can use the electricity when needed.

The largest electric eels in the world grow to a length of 10 feet. They are the most dangerous. But these eels are not found in the ocean. They are freshwater animals. They live in rivers in South America. So only divers in these rivers need to worry.

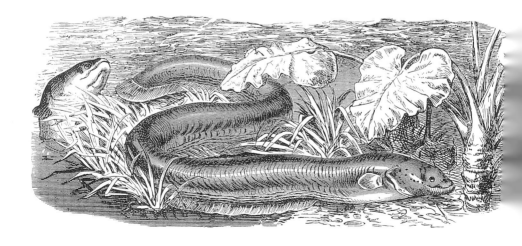

Are there other electric animals living in the water?

Yes. Eels are not the only fish that can make electricity. There are about 250 kinds of fish that can make electrical charges. None is as powerful as the electric eel.

Two other fish are also dangerous. They can produce electric shocks powerful enough to be a threat to humans.

One is the electric catfish. This fish is found in rivers in Africa.

The other fish is the electric ray. Electric rays live in the Atlantic Ocean and the Mediterranean Sea.

Chapter 3

More Danger Beneath the Waves

What nonliving dangers do you face in the water?

In the last chapter you learned about living dangers beneath the waves. But animals or other living things are not the only threats to a diver's safety. Danger can be as close as the water itself. Large waves, tides, or strong currents can kill. Let's learn more about these dangers.

How can waves bother you while you're scuba diving?

Divers must enter and leave the water safely. This is not always as easy as it sounds. If you are diving from a boat, it is very easy to get into the water. All you need to do is jump in. But getting back onto a boat can be a problem. The boat can be tossed about by large waves. The bigger the waves, the worse the problem becomes.

What if you plan to enter and leave the water from a beach? There can be similar problems. Large waves smashing against the beach can be very dangerous. They can easily slam a person into rocks, **pilings**, or other objects in the water.

Wave conditions must be studied very carefully BEFORE your dive begins. Find the safest path through the waves. Then follow it. Remember where you went in. You'll want to return the same way when your dive is over.

What makes currents so dangerous?

Currents are like rivers flowing through the ocean. They move huge amounts of water. Most people cannot swim against a strong current. So they must go wherever the water carries them.

Currents can become dangerous. They can carry divers away from the safety of their boats or the beach.

Be sure you know which direction the currents are moving the water where you plan to dive.

Why are tides dangerous?

Tides are changes in the level of the water. When the water level is high, it is high tide. When the water level is low, it is low tide. A change from high to low tide moves huge amounts of water. A diver can be carried along with this moving water.

As a diver, you must think about the tide BEFORE you enter the water. You must know if it is high or low tide. You need to know if the tide is coming in or going out. You need to know how the tide will change *during* your dive. If you don't understand tides, you may surface far away from the boat or beach.

Can you scuba dive at night?

You can scuba dive at night. But night dives create problems. Night diving is for skilled divers. It can be exciting. But it is also dangerous.

At night, you can see only as far as your flashlight allows. So when a night dive is necessary, always go with a buddy. Tie yourself to your partner with a 6- to 10-foot rope called a buddy line. Communicate with each other by tugging on the line.

Are there caves underwater?

Yes, there are underwater caves. There are also caves under the land that are flooded with water. Cave diving, like night diving, is for well-trained, skilled divers.

Caves can be very dangerous. If your air runs out inside a cave, you cannot just rise to the surface. There are no air spaces in some caves. If there is an air pocket, it can be dangerous. In some caves, this air is poisonous.

The diver must swim back to the cave entrance to come up for air. In a long, water-filled passageway, this may take too long. A diver could drown.

A cave diver must have special training.

Is the water always clear and easy to see through?

No. The water is not always crystal-clear. In lakes, ponds, rivers, and even in the ocean, the water can be dark and cloudy. This is usually caused by mud in the water. The mud makes it impossible for you to see more than a few feet. Sometimes you can see only a few inches in front of your mask. Diving in murky water is not a good idea.

Many dangers can lurk in muddy water. It is easy to swim into a sharp piece of metal or glass. If you cannot see it, you cannot avoid it. Sharp objects will cut your skin. They can also damage your diving gear.

In the darkness, you can become lost. You may not know which way is up. Even if you know the way, swimming to the surface in muddy water can be dangerous.

A diver must be careful not to come up under a boat or other object. A hard blow to the head can leave you unconscious. You could drown. To be safe, always hold a hand over your head as you come to the surface.

At the end of a dive, you must come to the surface. So anything that might hold you underwater after your air runs out is dangerous.

You could become tangled in ropes or wires. Such things are often thrown from a ship or pier. An old fishing net left in the water can trap you. Once you are trapped, it can be very hard to get free.

Many divers carry a special knife for emergencies. One edge of the blade is smooth and sharp. It is like a normal knife. The other edge of the blade is jagged, like a saw.

But just having a knife does not mean safety. A trapped diver may be able to free himself. His air might run out first, however.

If you have to dive in murky water, be very careful. Before going into the water, tie yourself to a diving partner with a buddy line. This may well be your lifeline!

Do people dive under frozen water?

Yes. You can learn to dive beneath ice. But it can be very dangerous. The water temperatures are very cold. You must wear a dry suit.

Ice divers have a problem that is similar to cave divers. In a cave, you must get back to the entrance. Under ice, you must find the hole where you came in. A safety line between you and a helper on the surface can solve this problem.

These are some of the dangers of diving. Most divers never meet all these dangers. But all divers meet some of them.

Chapter

A Walk or a Ride Beneath the Waves

How can someone walk underwater?

In the first chapter we learned about skin divers and scuba divers. But these are just two types of underwater workers and explorers. There are others.

Some are called hard-hat divers. A few use very special diving gear. One example is a **Jim suit**. A person cannot swim wearing this gear.

Divers using both hard hats and Jim suits must walk along the bottom.

What is hard-hat diving?

This diver wears a special hard helmet. The helmet is called a hard hat. It is usually attached to a diving suit. The suit is waterproof. The hard hat and suit help protect the diver.

The diver's air is pumped down from the surface. The air comes through hoses. The hoses are attached to the helmet.

Some of this air gets trapped in the helmet and suit. This makes the person float toward the surface.

But the diver needs to stay on the bottom. So he must wear a heavy belt and shoes. The belt and shoes have weights in them.

With so much weight, a hard-hat diver cannot move quickly and easily. He walks along the bottom of the ocean. He moves like an astronaut on the moon.

This diver is not free to swim to the surface. A hard-hat diver is lowered and raised by cables. The cables are attached to the suit. This kind of diving is not for fun. It is done by someone who works below the waves.

How deep can hard-hat divers go?

Some hard-hat divers breathe normal air. The air is pumped down to them from the surface. These hard-hat divers should go no deeper than scuba divers. They should not go below 130 feet.

With training, some hard-hat divers work at depths just over 200 feet. Other hard-hat divers breathe a special deep-diving gas mixture. These divers can go to a depth of 1,500 feet or more.

What is a Jim suit?

A Jim suit is a stiff, armored shell. Think of this suit as a walking **submarine**. It has two arms and two legs. It also has a large, round, insect-like head.

The diver stands inside this sturdy shell. There are four heavy, plastic ports or windows. They let the diver see the wet world outside.

The Jim suit gets its name from diver Jim Jarratt. He was the first person to wear one of these suits in 1935.

A diver might be very deep in the ocean. There may be several atmospheres of pressure in the water outside. But the Jim suit maintains one atmosphere of pressure on the inside. This is like flying in a jet. The air is pressurized to one atmosphere—just like the air on the ground.

The Jim suit lets the diver breathe the same air that you breathe. No special deep-diving gas mixtures are needed.

The suit has steel, robot-like hands attached. They can touch or hold objects outside the suit. The diver uses controls on the inside to move Jim's hands and fingers.

First, a diver is sealed safely inside the suit. Then the Jim suit is lowered by cable or carried to the ocean floor.

In 1976, a diver wearing a Jim suit was lowered from a ship. He went 1,440 feet down into the ocean. This took place off the coast of Spain. His job was to recover a TV cable.

In 1979, Sylvia Earle climbed into a Jim suit. She went down 1,250 feet. This was near Oahu, Hawaii.

She was strapped to the front of a **submersible** named *Star II*. Sylvia was not connected to the surface. She had a communications line attached to *Star II*. The submersible stayed close by her.

Now there's a new, lighter, less bulky suit. It is called a **NEWTSUIT**. This suit sometimes has small propellers. They help the diver move underwater.

In 1995, a NEWTSUIT was used to explore a shipwreck. The wreck was the cargo ship *Edmund Fitzgerald*. It rests on the bottom of Lake Superior.

The *Edmund Fitzgerald* sank on November 10, 1975. It is in Canadian waters, north of the state of Michigan.

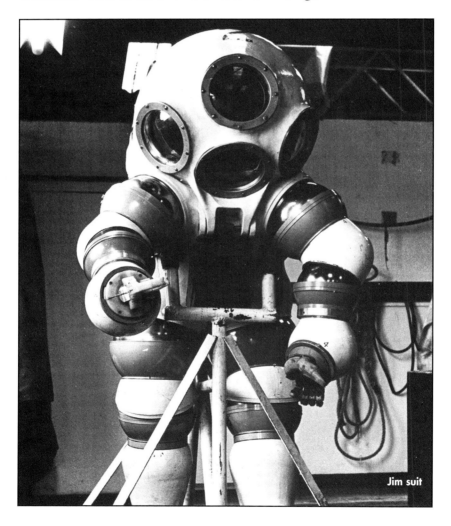

Jim suit

Alvin is a US Navy-owned deep submergence vehicle (DSV). *Alvin* can carry two scientists and a pilot to a depth of over 14,000 feet.

Is a submersible the same as a submarine?

The words *submerge* and *submerse* mean "to go below the surface." Submersible vehicles sometimes carry passengers underwater. They may also carry equipment underwater.

If the submersible carries people, it is said to be *manned*. A submarine is a submersible vehicle. But if the submersible carries only equipment, it is an *unmanned* vehicle.

There are three kinds of manned submersibles at work in the ocean. They are **mid-water drifters**, submarines, and **bathyscaphs**.

Who uses manned submersibles?

Manned, deep-diving submersibles have two main uses. They are used for scientific research or for deep-sea exploration.

Scientists who work in the ocean are called **oceanographers**. Oceanographers can use submersibles to study ocean animals.

Ocean animals live in the dark, cold world far below the surface. Scientists study these animals from the safety of their submersibles. They can even collect animals.

Scientists can also take samples of water, rocks, and mud. The samples are returned to the surface. Then they are carefully studied.

Most submersibles carry TV cameras and photo gear. The pictures let others see the exciting world miles below the waves. All this information helps us understand the ocean a little better.

Ocean scientists are not the only ones who use manned submersibles. These tiny submarines also perform secret military projects. They find and bring up valuable objects lost in deep water. They are also used to place special equipment on the ocean floor.

These submersibles have made it possible for people to reach every part of the deep ocean. But they are very costly to use. So governments and large companies often pay for the work submersibles do.

Why are unmanned submersibles needed?

There are many advantages to using unmanned submersibles. They are cheaper to build. And they are cheaper to use. With no one riding inside, costly life support gear isn't needed.

With no people aboard, these submersibles can stay underwater as long as the equipment works. This may be years.

Special unmanned submersibles are called **ROVs**. This name stands for *remotely operated vehicles.* They are controlled from a distance. A cable is attached to a ship or to a nearby manned submarine.

ROVs are moved around like remote-controlled toy cars. ROVs often have cameras. They can record what is in the water around them.

ROVs do many jobs underwater. They inspect oil pipelines or underwater cables. If the camera finds a problem, a person can be sent to fix it. ROVs find and recover costly equipment lost in the ocean.

Scientists use ROVs to gather important information. ROVs tell scientists about the water and the life that is in it.

How can submarines sink below the surface and come up again?

Boats are built to keep water out. But most submarines are built to let water in. Seawater can flow into special tanks inside a submarine. These tanks are called **ballast** tanks.

When the ballast tanks are filled with water, the submarine becomes heavy. It sinks beneath the waves.

When a submarine crew is ready to return to the surface, the water is pumped out of the ballast tanks. Air takes the place of the water. The submarine becomes lighter. It rises to the surface.

This is not the only way submarines move up and down in the ocean. Some use heavy weights to sink beneath the waves. When it is time to surface, the weights are dropped off. The submarine floats back to the top of the water.

What is a mid-water drifter?

The name says it all. This submersible is moved by the force of an ocean current. It **drifts** with the water.

The name also tells us where it drifts. This submarine does not move across the surface. Nor does it move across the bottom. It is carried in currents 300 to 2,500 feet below the surface. These submersibles drift along with mid-water currents.

The *Ben Franklin* is a well-known mid-water drifter. It once rode the powerful Gulf Stream Current north from the state of Florida all the way to New York.

How deep can submersibles go?

Each submersible is built so it can stand water pressure. But it can stand pressure only to a certain depth. By going deeper, the extra pressure could crush it.

Let's go down with a nuclear-powered U.S. Navy combat submarine. These large warships can safely dive about 1,500 feet below the surface.

Think about the 102-story Empire State Building in New York City. It stands 1,250 feet high. A Navy submarine can go that deep and more. It can go almost the length of a football field deeper. This is a long way down, right? Well, maybe not.

The average depth of the ocean is more than 2½ miles, or 13,600 feet. Suddenly, 1,500 feet does not seem so deep.

Other submersibles have been built to visit the truly deep-water world of inner space. They have much stronger, thicker sides.

One of the most famous submersibles is named *Alvin*. It can safely carry three people 13,000 feet below the surface.

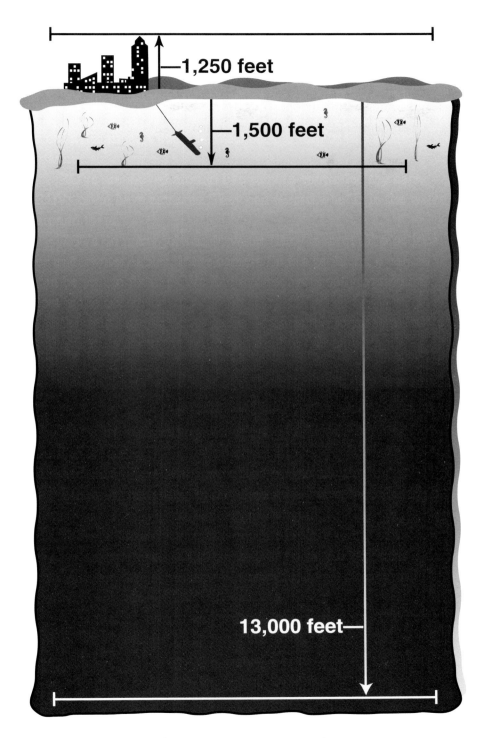

1,250 feet

1,500 feet

13,000 feet

Scientists rode *Alvin* down into the South Pacific Ocean. They went to study deep-ocean vents. Here they found many animals never-before seen.

Alvin also carried scientists 12,612 feet down in the North Atlantic Ocean. This trip was in 1989. Scientists inspected the wreckage of the *Titanic*.

The *Titanic* was a passenger ship. It had sunk 77 years earlier. The crew inspecting the wreckage carried along an ROV named *Jason Jr. Alvin* and the scientists could not go inside the sunken ship. But *Jason* could. *Jason* was attached to the end of a 200-foot-long cable.

The scientists used *Jason's* cameras as eyes. They moved *Jason* through the ship by remote control.

Other deep-water vehicles can go down farther than *Alvin*. In 1989, the Japanese submersible *Shinkai-6500* dove 21,320 feet.

This was the first submersible to go so deep and move so easily. It could go up and down. It could go forward and backward under its own power. The *Shinkai-6500* became the deepest-diving submarine in the world.

People can go even deeper. We can travel to the deepest place in the ocean. For this trip a bathyscaph is needed.

Bathyscaphs are made to travel easily up and down through the water. These vehicles have very little movement forward or backward. Because of this, bathyscaphs are not called submarines.

The following table shows the maximum safe diving depth for people. Compare the diving depths of people with two familiar ocean animals—the bluefin tuna and the sperm whale.

Jason is a remotely operated vehicle, (ROV).

WHOI

MAXIMUM SAFE DIVING DEPTHS

	Feet	Meters
Diver holding breath	100	30
Scuba (sport divers)	130	39
Hard-hat diver (breathing air)	218	66
Scuba (advanced training)	132	40
Bluefin tuna	600	183
Scuba (breathing special gas)	984	300
Jim suit (deepest dive)	1,440	439
Hard-hat diver (breathing special gas)	1,500	457
Sperm whale	3,000	915
Average depth of the ocean	13,612	4,150
Submarines		
U.S. Navy combat submarine	1,500	457
Deepstar 4,000	4,000	1,200
U.S. Navy DSRV	5,250	1,600
Beaver	6,000	1,800
Star III	6,500	2,000
Deep Quest	8,200	2,500
Alvin	13,000	4,000
Aluminaut	16,400	5,000
Shinkai-6500	21,320	6,498
Mid-water Drifter		
Ben Franklin	2,500	750
Bathyscaph		
Trieste	over 36,000	over 11,000

What is a bathyscaph?

A bathyscaph (BATH-uh-skaf) is the deepest-diving submersible in the ocean. The name *bathy* (deep) + *scaphe* (ship) tells us that this is a "ship of the deep."

The most well-known bathyscaph in the world is the *Trieste*. This submersible has two main parts. One is a small, thick-walled, hollow steel ball. The second is a large, cigar-shaped float. The ball is hung below the float.

The hollow ball is an observation sphere. It can carry only two people at a time. No one rides inside the float.

When the two-person crew is ready to dive, seawater is let in. The seawater fills ballast tanks in the float. The *Trieste* becomes heavy. It begins its long journey to the bottom.

At the end of the dive, the *Trieste* must return to the surface. This is done a little differently from most submersibles. The crew lets out tiny, solid iron balls. The balls have been held in large tubes inside the float.

By dumping out the iron balls, the *Trieste* becomes lighter. With less weight, it lifts off the bottom. It floats back to the surface.

In 1960, two men rode in the *Trieste* to the bottom of the Mariana Trench. This trench is in the western Pacific Ocean. It is the deepest place that has been found in any ocean. The water here is almost 7 miles deep! The round-trip ride took nearly nine hours. It took five hours to get to the bottom and four hours to float back to the surface.

What happens to people on a submarine that cannot get back to the surface?

The United States Navy has built a special submarine. It will rescue crew members trapped on a combat submarine. It is called a DSRV. That stands for *D*eep *S*ubmergence *R*escue Vehicle.

A DSRV can be attached to a stranded submarine. The crew can then climb aboard the DSRV. It will carry them to the surface.

But not all submarines are Navy warships. The stranded

crew of a smaller research vehicle could also have trouble. They may have no way out if their submarine becomes trapped far below the surface. A disaster in one of these submersibles could mean certain death for all the people on board.

This DSRV can be used for subsea rescues.

The ocean is beautiful. You can have lots of fun there. You can see interesting life. It is like another world. Don't be afraid to enjoy the ocean.

But remember to respect it. The ocean is not a natural environment for people. Use what you've learned in this book to protect yourself.

Maybe someday you will snorkel or scuba dive. You may even work for the Navy and go deep into the ocean. There are yet many things to learn there.

It is important to know about the ocean because it supports life on our planet. Perhaps you will be one of the lucky people who gets to study the ocean.

Whether you use the ocean for fun or study, remember to respect it and enjoy it!

GLOSSARY

apparatus
equipment put together for a special purpose

atmosphere
a measurement of pressure (about 15 pounds per square inch)

auditory tube
a tube that connects the inner ear and throat

ballast
anything heavy that is used to add weight to a submersible so that it will go underwater

bathyscaph
a manned vehicle for exploring the deepest depths of the ocean

buddy
a partner or companion

buoyancy compensator (BC)
makes up for any extra weight a diver is carrying. The BC makes the diver lighter and able to float in the water.

compressed
squeezed or pressed together

convulsion
a violent jerking of the body caused by the tightening of certain muscles

currents
horizontal movement of water

decompression
releasing from pressure

drift
carried along by water

gauge
an instrument for measuring the amount of something

great barracuda
a large, slender fish with a long, pointed head and knife-like teeth. It may grow 8–10 feet long and is found mostly in warm waters of the world.

jellyfish
a boneless, umbrella-shaped, jelly-like animal. It has stinging threads (called tentacles) that hang below the body.

Jim suit	a stiff, pressurized suit that keeps the diver at one atmosphere of pressure
mid-water drifter	a submersible that drifts with the current between the surface and the bottom
moray eel	a long, snake-like fish with narrow, long jaws and sharp, knife-like teeth. This fish has thick, slippery skin.
mouthpiece	the part of a snorkel or regulator that a person places in the mouth
neoprene	a man-made kind of rubber used to make wet suits
NEWTSUIT	a stiff diving suit used in deep water. It has propellers attached for easy movement
nitrogen	a gas without color, smell, or taste
oceanographers	(oh-shuhn-AH-gruh-furz) scientists who study the life, rocks, chemicals and movement of the ocean
oxygen	a gas without color, smell, or taste
piling	a large, wooden pole used to support a dock
sport diver	someone who dives for pleasure
regulator	something that controls the flow of gas from a tank to a diver
ROV	(remotely operated vehicle) an unmanned submersible that is controlled through a long cable by a person at another location
scuba	*Self-*Contained *U*nderwater *B*reathing *A*pparatus

shark	any of many different kinds of meat-eating fish. They have a tough hide and a skeleton made of cartilage. Sharks have small, tooth-like scales and five to seven gill slits on each side of their head.
stingray	flat-bodied fish related to sharks. They have a skeleton made of cartilage; small, tooth-like scales; and five to seven gill slits on each side of their head.
submarine	an underwater vehicle that can move easily up, down, forward, and backward under its own power
submersible	(sub-MER-sih-bull) a device for underwater work or research. This includes submarines and ROVs.
tentacles	(TEHN-tuh-kuhlz) long, thin extensions on a sea animal's body that are used for moving, feeling, stinging, or holding. Jellyfish have tentacles around their mouths for stinging.
tides	regular rise and fall of the ocean surface. This happens almost every 12 hours.
venom	a poisonous liquid forced into a victim by the bite or sting of some animals
weight belt	a special belt with weights attached. This is used to help a scuba diver sink beneath the surface.